GOD'S CALL / THE ⋯⋯⋯⋯⋯⋯⋯⋯⋯⋯ OSE

MENTOR GUIDE

Abingdon Press | Nashville

Affirm Mentor Guide

Writer: Jen Bradbury
Editor: Sara Galyon
Designer: Kent Sneed

Websites are constantly changing. Although the websites recommended in this resource were checked at the time this unit was developed, we recommend that you double-check all sites to verify that they are still live and that they are still suitable for students before doing an activity.

ISBN: 9781501867767
PACP10537572-01

18 19 20 21 22 23 24 25 26 27 — 10 9 8 7 6 5 4 3 2 1

MANUFACTURED IN THE UNITED STATES OF AMERICA

Contents

Meet the Writer

Jen Bradbury is a career youth worker who lives in the Chicago suburbs. She's the author of *Unleashing the Hidden Potential of Your Student Leaders*, *The Real Jesus*, and *The Jesus Gap*. When she's not writing or hanging out with teenagers, she enjoys reading, playing with her toddler, and traveling with her husband.

Introduction

As a youth pastor, one of the questions I hear most frequently from older adults in our congregation is, "Where are all the young people?"

Like it or not, there is a perception that once teens are old enough to choose for themselves whether they will participate in church, they'll make their way to the door. In some ways, research supports this perception. According to Fuller Youth Institute's College Transition Project, "40 to 50 percent of kids who are connected to a youth group when they graduate high school will fail to stick with their faith in college."[1] Researcher David Kinnaman suggests, "The dropout problem is, at its core, a faith-development problem; to use religious language, it's a disciple-making problem. The church is not adequately preparing the next generation to follow Christ faithfully in a rapidly changing culture."[2]

If the core of the dropout problem is a faith-development problem, then one of the best things the church can do is to disciple young people in their faith. One of the best ways to disciple young people in their faith is through one-on-one mentoring. That's why we're so excited about *Affirm*.

Affirm recognizes that faith is a journey and seeks to continue discipling teens in their faith after they've made their own decision to follow Jesus. The resource includes six sessions designed for a retreat or small-group setting and is meant to help teens continue to "affirm" their Christian faith and take their next steps in following Jesus. A vital part of *Affirm* is mentoring since faith is perhaps best modeled and learned in the context of relationships.

As a mentor, you'll spend six sessions investing in the faith formation of ONE young person. In the process, you'll learn and grow in your own faith as well.

The resource you're holding is the mentor guide for *Affirm*. Its six lessons correspond with each of the six lessons in *Affirm* that students will do together. It's meant to help teens go deeper in a one-on-one setting where they feel comfortable sharing.

Our hope is that with this guide, you'll feel equipped to mentor a teenager in his or her faith, knowing that what you're doing matters deeply—both in the teen's faith formation now and throughout his or her entire life. By mentoring a teen, you're helping your congregation get serious about discipleship and prepare the next generation to follow Jesus faithfully throughout their entire lives.

---

[1] From *Sticky Faith: Youth Worker Edition*, by Dr. Kara E. Powell, Brad M. Griffin, and Cheryl A. Crawford (Zondervan, 2011); page 15.

[2] From *You Lost Me: Why Youth Christians Are Leaving the Church . . . and Rethinking Faith,* by David Kinnaman (Baker Books, 2011); page 21.

The Role of the Mentor

When I began working as a youth worker, I knew I wanted to regularly meet one-on-one with students. I also knew I wanted to mentor one or two girls individually. After spending a few months getting to know the students, I was sure I wanted to mentor Jessica, a well-respected upperclassmen leader who was in a position of influence within our youth ministry and who longed to grow in her faith.

Much to my surprise, when I asked Jessica if she'd be open to meeting together, she eagerly agreed. So, we began meeting weekly to catch up on our lives and then discuss a chapter in a book we were each reading during the week. We would also pray together. This worked well for us. So well, in fact, that within a few months, I decided that everyone in our youth ministry needed to have a mentor.

Mentoring seemed like a great idea until I went to recruit my first mentor, whose immediate question was, "You want me to do what?!" That's when I realized that even though people are often familiar with mentoring in business, they're typically not used to the idea of spiritual mentoring.

Maybe that's you. Maybe you're familiar enough with the word *mentor* that when your senior pastor, a youth pastor, or even a student asked you to serve as a mentor for *Affirm*, you agreed. Then, later, you realized you didn't actually know what it meant to mentor. Rest assured, that's OK. You are not alone.

We wrote this mentor's guide for you. In it, you'll walk through the ins and outs of what it means to mentor a teenager. You'll learn practical how-to's that will equip you for your role. You'll also receive six weeks' worth of lessons that correspond with each week of the *Affirm* curriculum.

Mentoring in Business

So, what exactly is mentoring? In the business world, *mentor* has become a buzz word for one person investing in another to help him or her grow as a leader or in an area of competence. As such, a mentor can be seen as a critical path to success and many have identified their mentor as someone who has given them the skills that led to that success. As a formal structure, mentors are often assigned to mentees. As an informal process, mentees often must seek out their own mentors or those with experience seek out protégés to mentor.

Mentoring in the Church

If mentoring is viewed as a path to success in business, what then is spiritual mentoring?

Throughout Scripture, there are many examples of mentoring relationships. Jethro mentored Moses, Eli mentored Samuel, Jesus mentored his twelve apostles, and Paul mentored Timothy. In each instance, mentoring was about discipleship, building a relationship, and helping someone grow as a leader and develop his or her faith.

In his letter to the church at Thessalonica, Paul shared the following, "We were glad to share not only God's good news with you but also our very lives because we cared for you so much" (1 Thessalonians 2:8). In many ways, this is a good description of mentoring in the church: Sharing God's good news, sharing your life, and caring for someone. Sharing God's good news means that as a mentor you're doing something very specific: You're talking with your mentee about your faith and, in particular, God.

Because mentoring is a vehicle to form deep and lasting relationships in Christ, in a Christian mentoring relationship, you're not just being asked to connect socially or to develop a person's leadership skills. Rather, you're being asked to invest in the faith formation of another person and, in *Affirm*, a teenager. Doing so requires having intentional faith conversations, exploring Scripture, and praying together. The hard work of faith formation happens in the context of a relationship in which lives are shared with one another.

As you and your mentee share life together, you'll begin to care for and pray regularly for her or him throughout the mentoring journey. You'll provide support with your presence and care and by being a safe person with whom to express doubts and struggles.

Mentoring in Affirm

Chap Clark, a professor at Fuller Theological Seminary, talks often about reversing the 5 to 1 ratio in youth ministry. For a long time, it was considered a good practice to have one chaperone for every five teens in your ministry. But Chap asks, "What if we flipped that ratio upside down? What if we said we need five adults pouring into one kid?"[1] The first time youth workers hear this, they often panic as they envision a room full of five adult leaders for every one of their students. But that's not actually what Chap is saying.

Chap is saying that every teen needs five adults in addition to parents supporting him or her. By serving as a mentor, you gain the privilege of being an adult who relentlessly pursues and supports a teenager growing as a child of God. It's a sacred calling.

Now that we've covered what mentoring is, let's talk about what it's not. Mentoring is not parenting. Because you are not your mentee's parent, you occupy an almost liminal space with him or her that very few other adults occupy: one of trust. Your mentee may actually tell you things he or she would never share with parents and may be more honest with you than with parents, especially about matters of faith.

However, while you may become very influential in your mentee's faith journey, and maybe even in his or her life, you won't ever be as important as the parents (regardless of how often your teen tells you he or she doesn't respect, value, or appreciate them). This means you can't ever disparage your mentee's parents, even when it might be tempting to do so.

Mentoring also is not teaching; it's listening. Of course, as you mentor your teen, you will teach. However, others including parents, pastors, teachers, and youth ministry adult leaders will also teach your teen. Here's what differentiates you from them. Teachers are expected to be experts. They have some degree of authority on a particular subject matter. Their role as teachers also gives them positional authority over those they teach. When you mentor a teen, however, you're not operating out of a position of authority. You're not over your mentee; you're entering into a relationship *with* the teen.

Hopefully, this comes as good news to you, since you don't have to be a Bible expert, denominational guru, or theological scholar in order to mentor a teen. Why? Because even though you bring a wealth of life experience to your mentoring role, your primary role is not that of a teacher; your role is that of listener. Your job is to walk alongside and listen to the teen, meeting him or her wherever he or she is in the faith journey.

Instead of telling teens what to believe, you're helping them figure out what they actually believe. Instead of giving teens the answers to their questions, you're asking them more questions designed to prompt them to think seriously about their faith. As you do, you're discovering where your teen is in the faith journey and where you'll enter in, perhaps as a person willing to ask hard questions, sit with doubt, and share your story, as well as the places it intersects God's story. You're sharing not from a position of authority but rather as a fellow traveler on the journey of faith. You're doing so in a way that says, "I've been there too."

As you meet with your mentee, make it your goal to listen more than you talk. And as you listen, pay attention. Pay attention to how God is at work in your relationship with your student but also in the teen's life. After all, as Christians, we believe that God is living and active, that even now God is redeeming the world. One of the most important gifts you can give your mentee is to point out the ways in which God is moving in his or her life so that he or she can discover and join in God's kingdom work. You don't need Bible expertise, a specific degree, or even a history of church attendance to do that. You simply need to listen and point out what you see and hear. And to do that, you just need to be you.

So, with that in mind, THANK YOU for your willingness to jump into this scary, privileged role of mentoring. Know that what you're doing matters deeply in the life of your mentee . . . and we're guessing, in your own.

---

[1] From "Moving Away From the Kid Table," by Kara Powell (*https://fulleryouthinstitute.org/articles/moving-away-from-the-kid-table*).

Mentoring Safely

#MeToo.

It's a movement that spread virally in the fall of 2017 after repeated allegations surfaced about sexual misconduct and abuse by a number of high-profile celebrities and politicians. The movement began to gain mainstream attention when actress Alyssa Milano encouraged women to tweet #MeToo to demonstrate how many people have been affected by sexual misconduct and abuse.

Sadly, many in church congregations also came forward during this movement to share how they'd been sexually harassed and abused by pastors and adult leaders in positions of power. Such stories are a reminder of how important it is to enact and follow a child protection policy in your congregation. This is especially important anytime you meet with a student one-on-one, which, of course, is a vital part of mentoring.

Child Protection Policy

To protect you and your mentee, it's important for you to know and follow your congregation's child protection policy. This will ensure that you are above reproach and trustworthy when meeting with a teenager. It also ensures that teens are treated with the dignity that comes from being a beloved child of God.

Additionally, following your congregation's child protection policy will help you to develop a healthy relationship with your mentee. With that in mind, here are some specific guidelines to follow throughout the duration of your mentoring relationship:

- Meet, or at least call, a teen's parents before you begin mentoring. Explain what you want to do, where you'll be, and what you'll discuss. (*Note*: This is still a good practice even though you're mentoring someone as part of the *Affirm* curriculum and as a result, parents have hopefully heard about your role from your congregation's pastor or youth worker.)

- Always meet in public and never in a private place. This ensures there are always witnesses to your meetings. It may seem that this will hinder what teens are willing to share. However, they are used to having private conversations in public spaces at school and local gathering places. Meeting in public also puts you both on equal footing and power which is important for cultivating a relationship built on trust.

- Never give a teen a ride home unless there are multiple, unrelated people in the car with you at all times. Instead, choose a mutually agreed upon location to which teens can walk, ride a bike, drive, or get a ride.

- Be careful when communicating with teens via social media. Historically, as soon as a social media forum has been co-opted by parents (or people their parents' age), teens have found an alternative. Teens don't want to be friends with adults on social media; they want to inhabit these spaces with their peers. That's actually good for adults. Distancing yourself from teens on social media helps ensure your communication with them is above reproach. As a general rule, it's best to avoid social media when communicating with teens. Calling their home number and sending notes and cards via snail mail keeps the communication in a public forum. If you do use text or social media to communicate, keep it short and simple and limited to information only so that nothing can be misunderstood or misused.

- Although teens crave healthy physical touch, be careful with physical contact. Handshakes or high-fives are great ways to give good, comfortable physical touch to the teen you're mentoring. At times it can be appropriate to hug your mentee. However, don't initiate physical contact with your mentee. Instead, follow his or her lead.

The Importance of Confidentiality

Unless a teen can trust you, they won't share openly and honestly with you. Trust requires confidentiality. However, as an adult who's mentoring a teen, confidentiality cannot be taken lightly. In many states, clergy and those involved in the care of minors are "mandatory reporters"—people legally obligated to report certain things. As an adult working with teenagers, it is your responsibility to know the mandatory reporting laws in your particular state as well as your congregation's reporting procedure.

Regardless of whether you or the clergy in your church are mandatory reporters, be leery anytime a student asks you a question like, "If I tell you something, do you promise not to tell anyone else?" As a mentor, there are three instances in which you cannot keep confidential something a student tells you:

- If a student is being harmed;

- If a student is harming someone else;

- Or, if a student is harming him or herself.

Because of this, NEVER promise a student you'll keep confidential something he or she has told you or is about to tell you. Instead, promise to love, listen, support, care for, and do what is in his or her best interest.

If a student ever shares with you that he or she is being harmed, harming someone else, or harming self, report it (if applicable according to your state's laws) and tell the pastor or youth worker in your congregation about your conversation. You can do this in one of two ways:

1. Tell the pastor/youth worker about your conversation without your mentee present.

2. Go with your mentee to talk to your congregation's pastor/youth worker.

When a student is being harmed, harming someone else, or harming self, it involves adding people, not deleting them. This is especially important for you as a mentor. Once you've reported a situation to your congregation's pastor or youth worker, don't simply remove yourself from it. Instead, stay with the student. Continue to be a constant, caring, and supportive presence in the teen's life.

The Nitty-Gritty of Mentoring

You've just received a crash course in mentoring. Even so, you likely still have questions. Below are some of the most frequently asked questions by mentors as well as our answers to them.

How often should I meet with my mentee?

Relationships take time to develop. As a result, it's important to meet with your mentee regularly for several weeks. To decide exactly how often to meet, check with your congregation's pastor or youth worker to find out how they'll be using *Affirm*. Typically, *Affirm* will be used either in a retreat setting or as a small-group curriculum. If *Affirm* is being used in a retreat, then it would be ideal for mentors to meet with their mentees weekly for the six weeks following the retreat. If *Affirm* is being used in a small-group setting, then the ideal scenario is for mentors to meet with their mentees the week after the session is explored in small group.

When should I meet with my mentee?

The beauty of mentoring is that it's individualized. There's no specific day or time required for meeting. Instead, meet at a time that works for both of you. Depending on your schedule, it might work best to meet with your mentee over the weekend or on a weeknight, setting up a regular meeting time and place. Or, you might find it best to evaluate your schedule on a weekly basis. If that's the case, each time you meet, schedule your next meeting.

How long should we meet?

Again, both you and your mentee can decide but, in general, an hour is adequate. This gives you time to grab food, catch up on your week together, discuss the week's lesson (which is included in this book), and pray together.

Where should I meet with my mentee?

Teens like food. Let's face it, adults do too. So, you might find it helpful to meet with your mentee while eating. (Eating is also something you can do together.) Choose a favorite coffee shop, ice-cream parlor, or fast-food restaurant and meet there. Alternatively, you might discover that you and your mentee talk better if you're actively doing something. If so, schedule a round of Frisbee golf or take a walk together. The only constraint on where you meet is that it needs to be a public place, according to your church's safety policy as discussed earlier.

What's important is that you commit to actually talking before, during, or after your activity. Doing something together is great for forming relationships. However, we want your time together to be about faith formation as well.

What should we do when we meet?

Eat, talk, and listen.

Seriously, that's it.

However, even that can sound daunting. Because we know that, we've included six lessons in this mentor guide, each corresponding to a lesson in *Affirm*. These lessons are meant to include everything you need to have a good meeting with your mentee. However, YOU are the expert on your teen. Feel free to add or delete questions from these lessons so that they work for you and your mentee.

What should we bring to our meetings?

You'll need only two items for your mentoring meetings: this book and a Bible. Aside from that, you already have everything else you need to mentor your teen: a love of God, a heart for teenagers, a willingness to listen, and a desire to share your personal faith journey with someone else.

Exactly how long of a commitment am I making?

As a mentor for *Affirm*, we're asking you to commit to meeting with your mentee six times to work through the corresponding *Affirm* lessons. After that our hope is that if there's chemistry, and you and your mentee want to continue in a formal mentoring relationship, you'll do so. Otherwise, we hope you'll continue to invest in your mentee in other ways. (We'll give you some suggestions for how to do that in the last chapter of this book.)

Mentoring Lessons

We want to make it as easy for you to mentor your mentee. For that reason, this mentor guide includes six lessons, each corresponding to one lesson in *Affirm*. Each mentoring lesson includes five parts as described below.

Tip of the Week

Affirm mentors are not expected nor required to have any mentoring knowledge or experience. However, we want to set you up for success. With that in mind, each week's lesson begins by offering you a simple tip to help you and your mentee have a positive experience.

Lesson Summary

As an *Affirm* mentor, you aren't expected nor required to attend the *Affirm* retreat or small groups (unless your youth pastor or *Affirm* leader requires it). However, we want you to know what happened there. So, each lesson contains a summary of the corresponding *Affirm* lesson. While the lessons in this guide are designed to accompany and even compliment the lessons in *Affirm*, they're not repeats of what your mentee has already discussed during *Affirm*. Instead, we want you to expand upon and go deeper into the information that's already been taught.

Catch-up Questions

Each time you meet with your mentee, you should spend a few minutes simply catching up on your week together. You may do this in a variety of ways, but we'll include one specific idea in each lesson. Feel free to repeat an idea if one works better than others with your mentee.

Discussion Questions

Discussion questions form the bulk of your lesson. Many of the discussion questions are personal in nature. That's the beauty of a one-on-one mentoring relationship. It is an opportunity to go deep with another person.

The weekly discussion questions also will introduce a short Bible passage for you to explore with your mentee. This Bible passage is related to the week's theme, but it is not one teens have already explored during *Affirm*. Our hope is that studying a different passage will enable your mentee to gain a broader understanding of what Scripture says about a particular topic.

We've designed each lesson to fill sixty minutes. If you schedule your mentoring meetings to last one hour, we don't anticipate you'll need to *add* anything to the material that's provided. However, YOU are the expert on your mentee. If there's a question you think would be helpful, please include it in your discussion! If you're confident one of the questions won't work for your teen, then don't use it.

As you talk about these questions with your mentee, focus on the quality of your conversation, not the number of questions you discuss. We've included adequate material so that you don't feel pressured to add questions or end up sitting in awkward silence. However, some weeks will resonate with your teen more than others. Additionally, some weeks your teen will be more talkative than others. So, if your conversation is going great and you only talk about a few of the questions, that's OK. You've done your job and done it well! But if your conversation is moving slower and you need to discuss all of the questions, that's OK too! You are not a failure. You've still done your job and done it well!

Closing Prayer

The conclusion of each lesson is a closing prayer prompt. Of course, you're welcome to include prayer throughout your time together with your mentee. We also hope you'll take time to regularly pray for your mentee throughout this process. However, we want you to intentionally end your time together in prayer.

Prayer is one of those things that different people are comfortable doing in different ways. Some people love to pray aloud. Others prefer to pray silently. Some people love to compose their prayers in the moment. Others prefer to pray using the words of others. All of these are good ways to pray.

What we'd like you to do most with your mentee is practice conversational prayer together. As a result, the closing prayer prompts included in these lessons are meant to be more conversational (and relational) in nature. For some of you, that might be a stretch. That's OK.

As you pray, remember that you don't have to be a pastor to pray. Teens won't judge you or grade your prayers. In fact, even if you stumble through your prayers, they will still be a blessing to your mentee. Teens don't often have adults in their lives who pray with them regularly, so your willingness to pray with your mentee is invaluable.

You also don't need to be the only one who's praying. Encourage your mentee to pray too! When your teen joins in the prayer, affirm her or his words and, when applicable, the messiness of the prayers.

Mentoring Lesson 1: The Faith Journey

Tip of the Week: Prepare Well

Imagine this. You realize it is the night before your first meeting with your mentee. That realization sends you into a panic. Remember, if you love God and have a heart for teenagers, you'll be a great mentor—as long as you prepare.

Teens are not used to having conversations with adults. They're used to being lectured or taught. As a result, you can't expect to sit down in your first mentoring meeting and have your mentee talk nonstop for the next hour. That simply won't happen.

To prepare for your mentoring meeting, spend time in prayer, calming your heart and mind. Then spend time praying for your mentee by name. As you get to know your mentee better, allow your prayers for him or her to become more specific.

After you've prayed, read the relevant mentoring lesson, along with the related Bible passages. Highlight or underline key words or phrases so that when you glance at the pages, you'll quickly be able to skim the question and know what you're supposed to ask. Think through how you'd answer each of the discussion questions. Jot down notes to help you remember important parts of your answer. Contemplate potential follow-up questions to take the conversation deeper and make note of those as well. Some mentors find it helpful to rewrite the discussion questions. The act of slowly rewriting them often helps to internalize them, making discussion more conversational.

If possible, spend a few minutes the day of your mentoring meeting reviewing the lesson, Scriptures, and your notes. It's

OK to take this book with you to the meeting. No one expects you to have every aspect or question memorized. However, you should be familiar enough with the content that you aren't glued to the page.

After your mentoring meeting concludes, spend a few minutes reflecting on what aspects did and didn't go well. Then decide what you need to tweak in preparation for your next mentoring meeting.

Lesson Summary:

Transformation is a process; it's part of a journey to becoming more like Christ. While parts of the journey must be traveled alone, the journey cannot be completed without the involvement of fellow travelers. During this session in *Affirm*, students explored their pace of transformation and learned how it is unique to the purpose God has for them. They also wrestled with the role the community of faith plays in supporting and encouraging them along the way. The anchor point for this session was Philippians 1:6:

> "I'm sure about this: the one who started a good work in you will stay with you to complete the job by the day of Christ Jesus."

Catch-up Questions:

Your role as a mentor is to develop a relationship with your mentee. To help you develop a relationship, begin your time together by simply catching up on the previous week.

This week catch up by sharing your highs and lows. Share a highlight as well as a low point from the past week. Ask your mentee to do the same.

Consider closing your catch-up time in prayer by praying for the highs and lows you and your partner shared.

Discussion Questions:

Spend the majority of time together with your mentee discussing and, in some instances, wrestling with the following discussion questions.

1. What is the best journey you've ever taken?

2. What must you do to prepare for a journey?

3. How, if at all, is faith like a journey?

4. Who or what has prepared you for your journey of faith?

5. Where would you say you are currently in your faith journey: the beginning, middle, or end? Why?

6. When, if ever, have you felt stuck in your journey of faith?

7. How has your journey of faith changed over time?

8. In general, is change easy or hard for you? Why do you think this is true?

9. What grade were you in a year ago? How were you different? What extracurricular activities filled your time? Who were your closest friends? What was important to you? What did you do most often in your spare time?

10. What's happening in your life now? What grade are you in? What extracurricular activities fill your time? Who are your closest friends? What's important to you? What do you do most often now in your spare time?

11. How have you changed since last year? Do you think these changes are positive or negative? Why?

12. If you were to ask your parents how you've changed since last year, what do you think they'd say? Would they say you've experienced positive or negative changes? Why?

13. Think about your life throughout the past several years. What are some of the most significant periods of change you've experienced? What prompted those changes? In retrospect, were those changes positive or negative? Why?

14. What, if any, role has God played in the changes you've experienced in your life over the last few years? Is God's role only in changing your faith, or do you think God is involved in other changes in your life also? Why?

15. Now think about your faith. What three words would describe your faith a year ago? What three words describe your faith today? How has your faith changed during the past year?

16. Would you say your faith today is stronger or weaker than it was a year ago? Why?

17. Read 2 Corinthians 5:17. What do you think it means to be "in Christ"? Are you "in Christ"? Why or why not?

18. How has your faith in Jesus made you a "new creation"?

19. What "old things" have gone away as you've matured in your faith? How has this changed you?

20. A year from now, how do you want to be able to describe your journey of faith? In order to describe your faith journey in that way, what must you do or change between now and then?

Closing Prayer

This week, as you close in prayer:

- Pray that your mentee would experience God in the midst of all the changes of his or her daily life.

- Ask God to help your mentee see him or herself as a loved, forgiven "new creation."

- Pray that your mentee will have the courage to continue growing in the journey of faith.

- Ask God to help your mentee take the steps needed to grow in faith.

After praying for your mentee, give him or her the opportunity to pray for you as well.

Mentoring Lesson 2: The Faith Given to You

Tip of the Week: Share Your Story

One of the unique aspects of mentoring is that it's a two-way street. That's why we've written the mentoring lessons as discussions rather than bulleted lists of talking points. Notice, however, the word we used here: *discuss.*

That's important.

These lessons are written as discussions and not sermons or outlines, because you shouldn't be the one doing all the talking. Remember, your job as a mentor is more about listening than teaching. However, teenagers never want to be interrogated—ever. Interrogations cause teens (well . . . anyone) to feel uncomfortable. Teens feel like you're searching for a right answer rather than entering into their faith journey as a co-doubter who is committed to walking with them throughout their faith journey.

So, even though you shouldn't dominate the conversation, as a mentor, you also shouldn't be silent. Instead, share parts of your story so that teens feel comfortable sharing theirs. As you share your story, carefully consider the details you divulge. In an effort to connect with teens, adults tend to over share, revealing information that should only be shared with other adult friends. (And to be clear, a mentee is NOT your friend. Teens don't need more friends in their lives. They need adults who care about them.) To help you consider what details to share with a teenager, first ask yourself, *For whose benefit am I sharing this?* Only share details with a student if you're genuinely doing so for his or her benefit.

As you share stories with your mentee, be aware of your tone. Since you're an adult, mentees will automatically consider you more like their parents. They'll expect you to lecture them. So, surprise them! Establish a "Me, too" tone rather than an authoritative one. Share stories as a fellow traveler on the journey of faith, someone who's been there before, not as someone who has it all figured out.

To that end, don't be afraid to say "I don't know" to your mentee. As someone who's primary job is listening, not teaching, there is no expectation for you to know it all. So, don't fake it until you make it. Instead, be honest about what you do and don't know. If you don't know something, admit it. Then commit to searching for the answer together with your mentee, perhaps by exploring Scripture together or finding someone else who knows the answer.

Remember, the best mentor/mentee relationships are ones in which both people learn from each other. Sharing your story allows you to come alongside your mentee as a fellow learner.

Lesson Summary

We do not come to faith on our own. We have others who teach us about God and show us what it means to live out our faith. Ultimately, however, having faith in God is a personal commitment that requires individuals to make decisions about what they believe and how they will live out that belief.

This week in *Affirm*, students considered the question, "Where does your faith come from?" This lesson helped students think more deeply about who has influenced their faith and whose faith they will influence.

The anchor point for this session was 1 Corinthians 3:5-6:

> "After all, what is Apollos? What is Paul? They are servants who helped you to believe. Each one had a role given to them by the Lord: I planted, Apollos watered, but God made it grow."

Catch-up Questions

Your role as a mentor is to develop a relationship with your mentee. To help you develop a relationship, begin your time together by catching up on the previous week. To do this, consider the following question:

What's one gift you received during the past week? Remember: Gifts are not always tangible. They also can be intangible.

After your mentee has shared, share your answer to this question as well. Then consider closing this time together in prayer.

Discussion Questions

Spend the majority of time together with your mentee discussing and, in some instances, wrestling with the following questions.

1. We know from biology that we inherit half of our DNA from our mothers and half from our fathers. Is faith inherited in the same way as DNA? Why or why not? If not, how is our faith passed on to us?

2. Earlier you were asked to tell about a gift you received this week. Do you think the faith you've been given is a gift? Why or why not?

3. Who has most influenced your faith? Why?

4. What have you learned from your faith influencers about faith? How, if at all, do you hope your faith will look like theirs?

5. What have you learned from your parents about faith? How, if at all, do you hope your faith will look like theirs?

6. What have you learned from our church about faith? Why? What, if anything, do you wish you'd learned from our church that you haven't? Why?

7. Which of your beliefs or faith traditions do you wish you hadn't inherited? Why? Without these beliefs or faith traditions, how would your faith be different?

8. How have you made your faith your own? In other words, how does your faith look different from that of your parents or our church?

9. Read Matthew 7:24. What makes someone a "wise builder"? What skills are necessary to be considered a "wise builder"?

10. Read Matthew 7:25. What must a house be built on in order to withstand storms? Now relate this to your faith. What are some of the storms you have encountered or might encounter in your journey of faith?

11. For your faith to withstand the inevitable storms you'll encounter, what must be its foundation? Do you currently feel as though your faith is built on that foundation? Why or why not?

12. Think about the faith you've inherited. How solid is the foundation of your faith? Why?

13. Read Matthew 7:26-27. There's only so much you can do about the faith you've inherited. What, if anything, can you do to strengthen a poor foundation of faith?

14. If a storm hit your faith right now, would your faith be able to withstand it? Why or why not?

15. Practically speaking, what can you do to create a stormproof faith?

16. Whose faith have you influenced? Why?

17. As you influence the faith of others, how can you become a wise builder?

18. If you don't yet feel as though you've influenced the faith of others, what could you do or change to be someone who's able to influence others' faith?

19. Imagine your life as an adult. If you have kids, what do you hope they'll be able to say about your faith? What can you do NOW to help you get to the point where your future kids would be able to say that about your faith?

Closing Prayer

This week, as you close in prayer:

- Pray by name for those who have influenced your mentee's faith. Thank God for the ways in which your mentee's faith has been influenced by those people.

- Pray for your mentee's parents. Thank God for the ways in which your mentee's parents have influenced her or his faith.

- Pray for your congregation. Thank God for the ways your church body has influenced your mentee's faith.

- Ask God to continue to strengthen the foundation of your mentee's faith.

- Commit to God any steps your mentee has agreed to take to stormproof her or his faith. Ask God to bless these steps and to use them to strengthen your mentee's faith.

Once you've prayed for your mentee, give him or her the opportunity to pray for you as well.

Mentoring Lesson 3: Life in Christ

Tip of the Week: Listen Well

You already know that your primary role as a mentor isn't teaching; it's listening. But what does it mean to listen well? Listening well means not talking when another person is talking. However, it doesn't mean not responding. In fact, good listeners are active listeners, not only with your ears but also with your eyes and the entire body.

Listening well requires making eye contact with the person who's talking. It also means giving nonverbal cues that you're paying attention. Good nonverbal cues include shaking the head in agreement and leaning forward to truly hear what someone's saying.

Listening well also means paying attention to your body language. Sitting with your arms crossed can be perceived as being closed off. The same is true of leaning backwards, as though trying to remove yourself from a situation.

In addition to actively listening, good listeners also engage verbally. Repeating what you've heard helps someone feel as though you've listened well and gives an opportunity to correct anything you may have misheard. Asking questions shows you're interested and want to learn more.

Another sign of active listening is affirming what you hear. As mentor, you're asking your mentee to trust you. To encourage your teen to share with you, affirm what you hear. This doesn't mean you have to agree with everything your mentee says. In fact, you shouldn't. As a caring adult you need to tell the truth.

Even if you disagree with what your mentee says, thank your mentee for sharing it with you, for entrusting you with the story. Remind your mentee that unless something like being hurt, hurting someone else, or hurting self has been shared, the information will stay with you. You won't report it to parents, a youth worker, or friends.

Lesson Summary

This week in *Affirm*, your mentee considered the questions, "Who do you resemble?" and "How is your life a reflection of God?" This lesson challenged students to consider the many characteristics of God and how they embody those characteristics to reflect the divine image. The anchor point for this lesson was Galatians 5:22-23:

> "But the fruit of the Spirit is love, joy, peace, patience, kindness, goodness, faithfulness, gentleness, and self-control. There is no law against things like this."

Catch-up Questions

To catch up with your mentee this week, use this question:

What groups are you involved in at school? Why did you decide to become involved in those groups?

After your mentee has answered these questions, tell about some of the work or community groups in which you participate and why you chose to be involved in them.

Discussion Questions

Spend the majority of time together with your mentee discussing and, in some instances, wrestling with the following questions:

1. When is a time you felt like you belonged and a time when you felt as though you didn't?

2. In general, what makes you feel like you belong?

3. Do you feel as though you belong to our church? Why or why not?

4. At confirmation, you affirmed your faith and officially became a member of our church. How, if at all, did your sense of belonging change after you were confirmed?

5. Read 1 Corinthians 12:12-14. How is the body of Christ (the church) like a human body?

6. Think about the church today. Do you think the church acts as though it's ONE body or many bodies? Why? What about our church? Do you think our church acts as though it's one body or many bodies? Why?

7. Read 1 Corinthians 12:15-16. Who do you think Christians today wish weren't a part of the body of Christ? Based on this passage, do you think Paul, the author of 1 Corinthians, would say this group is a part of the body of Christ? Why or why not?

8. What would our church have to do in order to welcome those who Christians wished weren't a part of the body of Christ into OUR congregation? What would we risk by doing so? gain?

9. First Corinthians 12:16 imagines that an ear might say, "I'm not part of the body because I'm not an eye." Describe a time when you wished you WEREN'T part of the body of Christ. Why did you feel that way?

10. Based on 1 Corinthians 12:16, do you or the body decide whether or not you're a part of the body? Why?

11. Read 1 Corinthians 12:17-20. How are the people who belong to our church similar? different?

12. What might we lose if everyone in our church were the same?

13. What might our church learn from people who are different from us?

14. Read 1 Corinthians 12:21-22. Who might Christians label as the "weakest" parts of the body? What about in our congregation? Who might people label as the "weakest" parts of our body?

15. Read 1 Corinthians 12:23-25. What do you think causes division in the church? What, if anything, has or is causing division in our congregation? Why?

16. What are the different "parts" of our congregation?

17. How can the different "parts" of our congregation show mutual concern for one another? Practically speaking, what would it look like for the youth ministry to show mutual concern for the music ministry?

18. Read 1 Corinthians 12:26. How are people in our congregation currently suffering? Practically speaking, how can we suffer with them? How can suffering together create a sense of belonging? Who in our congregation is currently getting the glory? How can we celebrate with them? How might celebrating one another's accomplishments create a sense of belonging?

19. Read 1 Corinthians 12:27. Do you think our youth ministry behaves as though we're the body of Christ? Why or why not? How can we do a better job?

20. Why is being part of the body of Christ important? How might being part of the body of Christ be important in your future life, especially during times of doubt and suffering?

Closing Prayer

This week, as you close in prayer:

- Pray for the various groups to which your mentee belongs. Thank God for the role they play in your mentee's life and that of your community. Ask God to meet the needs of these groups.

- Pray that your mentee would experience a true sense of belonging, both inside and outside the walls of the church.

- Pray for unity amongst the body of Christ.

- Pray for those in your community who are suffering.

- Pray for those in your community who are celebrating.

- Ask God for the courage to suffer and celebrate with those currently doing either.

- Pray that your mentee would understand how important it is to be part of the body of Christ, imperfect though it might be.

Once you've prayed for your mentee, give him or her the opportunity to pray for you as well.

Mentoring Lesson 4: Know What You Believe

Tip of the Week: Adding and Deleting

By now you're starting to know a little bit about your mentee, what he or she is passionate about and what makes him or her tick. You're also probably beginning to sense which discussion questions will and won't work with your mentee. With that in mind, think specifically about what you might want to add and delete from these lessons. Take time to think through how you might modify the discussion questions to make them work better for your particular mentee.

If, after the first three lessons, you've realized you can't cover all the material, begin planning for what you can skip. As you read through the discussion questions, mark with an S (for skip) those questions you think are less interesting. Then take a second pass through the discussion questions and also mark those questions you think won't connect well with your mentee. Then, during the actual meeting, you won't have to think about which questions to skip. Also, if you're running short on time, you can skip any questions marked with an S.

Similarly, if after the first three lessons you've consistently run out of questions to discuss with your mentee, spend some time thinking of specific follow-up questions. Follow-up questions can go deeper on a subject, or they can tie directly to something you've been talking about with your mentee in previous weeks. Trust your instincts. You are the expert on meeting with your particular student!

Lesson Summary

Most teenagers will know someone in their circle of friends, relatives, or neighbors who does not believe God matters. Part of growing in faith is being able to explain to others why God matters and the difference God makes in our lives. In this *Affirm* lesson, students explored why God's love matters most and why God's love matters to them. The anchor point for this lesson was Ephesians 2:8-9:

> "You are saved by God's grace because of your faith. This salvation is God's gift. It's not something you possessed. It's not something you did that you can be proud of."

Catch-up Questions

To catch up with your mentee this week, use this prompt:

Tell me about a time in the past week when you disagreed with someone. Why did you disagree? How did you handle this disagreement? How, if at all, did your faith influence your understanding of the issue at hand OR your treatment of the person with whom you disagreed?

After your mentee has answered, share your response to the catch-up prompt as well.

Discussion Questions

Spend the majority of time together with your mentee discussing and, in some instances, wrestling with the following questions:

1. If you could ask God one question, what would it be, and why?

2. How do you imagine God responding to your question? Why? What does this suggest about your perception of God's character?

3. What has caused you to doubt God's love?

4. What, if anything, could you do to make God love you less? to make God love you more? Why?

5. How does Jesus' death demonstrate God's love?

6. Read John 15:9-10. What does it mean to remain in God's love?

7. Read John 15:11-12. What does it mean to love one another in the same way Jesus loved us? How can we do this in practical ways?

8. Recall the disagreement you mentioned earlier. How can you love this person in the way Jesus loved you?

9. Read John 15:13. Is Jesus truly saying you should be willing to die for your friends? Why or why not?

10. Do you have any friends you would be willing to die for? If so, who? Under what circumstances?

11. Aside from dying for your friends, how can you sacrifice yourself for the benefit of your friends?

12. Do you think believing in God matters to our lives NOW, or do you think believing in God is more about what happens after we die? Why?

13. How, if at all, does believing in God matter to your life now?

14. Describe a time when you thought God didn't matter. Why did you feel that way?

15. How might a good Christian community remind you that your faith matters, even during times when it's hard to believe God matters?

16. Do you think you have a Christian community that can remind you of the difference God makes in life?

If so, tell about a time this community reminded you that God matters. If not, what would it take to find and form a Christian community to do that for you?

17. Imagine if someone from your school were to ask you, "What does it mean to be a Christian?" What would you tell them? Why?

18. What are common beliefs shared by all Christians, beliefs without which you could no longer say, "I'm a Christian"?

Closing Prayer

This week, as you close in prayer:

- Pray for resolution of the disagreement your mentee shared earlier.

- Pray that your mentee would experience God's love in an undeniable way.

- Ask God to give your mentee the courage to love people—even during disagreements—in the same way Jesus loves them.

- Pray that your mentee would come to know and understand why God matters now in her or his life, not just after death.

- Ask God to surround your mentee with Christian friends to remind him or her that God matters today.

- Pray that your mentee will continue wrestling with what it means to be a Christian.

After you've prayed for your mentee, give him or her the opportunity to pray for you as well!

Mentoring Lesson 5: Know Why You Believe

Tip of the Week: Push Back

I once interviewed a college student for a research project I was working on who asked, deadpan: "Can't I just answer 'Jesus' for everything? Jesus is always the right answer in church, isn't he?"

Like this student, teens who have grown up in the church know that Jesus is ALWAYS the right answer. In the course of attending church week after week, teens have learned how to speak Christianese—the language of Christians. They can throw around phrases such as, "Jesus died for our sins" often enough to make us believe they actually understand what it means.

The problem is that learning a language starts with repeating what you hear, not necessarily understanding what you're saying. Even though teens might speak Christianese fluently, they don't always know what they're saying.

As a mentor in a one-on-one environment, you have the unique opportunity to push back on what teens say to help them think through what they believe and why, a process that gives them ownership of their faith. Always push back during your mentoring meetings with teens. As they respond to your questions, always ask, "Why?" Asking why forces them to actually think through why (or if) they believe something rather than merely repeating it. If a teen cannot answer why, help them do so. Investigate relevant Scripture passages together and offer your reason(s) for believing something.

Similarly, if you suspect teens are just repeating what they've been taught, call them out by asking, "Is that what YOU actually believe, or is that what your parents (or pastor or youth pastor) have told you?" Directly asking teens this question gives you an opportunity to engage them in a meaningful conversation about the process of making their faith their own (rather than simply accepting their inherited faith, the latter of which rarely holds up when teens are faced with crises or direct challenges to their faith).

Also, occasionally you can push back against what teens say by playing devil's advocate. When you play devil's advocate, share a perspective that counters the one teens are suggesting. Hearing a different perspective helps broadens their thinking and, again, enables them to decide what they actually believe and why. You can play devil's advocate even if you don't necessarily agree with the perspective you're proposing. To do so, begin by saying: "Not everyone would agree with what you just said. How would you respond to someone who suggested . . .?"

The goal of playing devil's advocate is to help teens think, not to make them feel terrible for the belief they hold. Use this practice thoughtfully in moments when you suspect teens are simply regurgitating information they've repeatedly heard from others. Doing so strengthens their faith by forcing them to decide for themselves what they believe and why.

Lesson Summary

Having established a firm foundation of belief in God's love, this lesson in *Affirm* explored God's expectations for what we are meant to do with that love.

The anchor point for this lesson was Matthew 25:21:

> "His master replied, 'Excellent! You are a good and faithful servant! You've been faithful over a little. I'll put you in charge of much. Come, celebrate with me.'"

Catch-up Questions

To catch up with your mentee this week, use this prompt:

Tell me about a time last week when you had to defend something, perhaps a decision you made or a position you held. To whom did you have to defend this? What reasoning did you use to defend your position? Were you able to defend your position without becoming defensive? Why or why not?

After your mentee answers, share your response to the catch-up prompt also.

Discussion Questions

Spend the majority of time together with your mentee discussing and, in some instances, wrestling with the following questions:

1. How easy or difficult is it for you to talk about your faith with your friends from church? with your family? with your friends at school?

2. Is sharing your faith with your friends the same thing as inviting them to church? Why or why not? For you, which is easier? Why?

3. For you, what's hardest for you when talking about your faith with friends at school?

4. What would you need to do or know in order to become more comfortable talking with your friends about your faith?

5. Read 1 Peter 3:15. What is your hope? How does your faith in Jesus give you hope?

6. First Peter 3:15 says, "Whenever anyone asks you to speak of your hope . . .." How often do people ask you to speak of your hope or of your faith? Under what circumstances is faith usually a topic of conversation?

7. What, if anything, do you think you could do to make people more likely to ask you about your hope in Jesus?

8. First Peter 3:15 commands us to "be ready to defend" the hope that we have. To you, what does it mean to defend someone or something?

9. Do you think it's possible to defend someone or something without becoming defensive? Why or why not?

10. In order to "be ready to defend" the hope you have, what must you know or be willing to do? Why?

11. How can you actually prepare to talk about your faith with others? What might you gain from doing so?

12. Imagine if someone were to ask you why you spend a week at church summer camp or serving on a mission trip. How might you use this as an opportunity to "defend" the hope that you have?

13. When it comes to your faith, of what belief(s) are you most confident? Why?

14. How might you "defend" the belief you're most sure of to someone who asks you about church?

15. This week in *Affirm* you talked about accountability. What is the meaning of *accountability* to you?

16. Read Hebrews 12:1-2. How is faith like a race?

17. What does it mean to fix your eyes on Jesus? Practically speaking, what does it look like to fix your eyes on Jesus?

18. How might having someone hold you accountable to run your race enable you to fix your eyes on Jesus?

19. We've spent the last several weeks together in a mentoring relationship. How, if at all, does our mentoring relationship give you accountability? Should it give you more accountability? Why or why not?

20. When it comes to your faith, what's one thing for which you need someone to help hold you accountable? How can I do that for you?

Closing Prayer

This week, as you close in prayer:

- Thank God for the hope you have in Jesus.

- Pray for those who have the courage to ask your mentee about his or her faith.

- Ask God to give your mentee the courage and the words to defend his or her faith to those who are interested in hearing more.

- Pray for your mentee to have confidence in what she or he believes and why.

- Ask God to give your mentee someone (perhaps you!) the ability to hold him or her accountable for growing in faith and fixing his or her eyes on Jesus.

Once you've prayed for your mentee, give him or her the opportunity to pray for you also.

Mentoring Lesson 6: Hearing God Speak

Tip of the Week: Tangential Conversations

As you meet with your mentee, inevitably some of your conversations won't go exactly as planned. A question might prompt a completely tangential conversation. When this happens, mentors often worry about what to do.

First of all, don't panic. Tangents aren't bad. In fact, tangents are actually good. They show students are engaged in the conversation.

When you're teaching a room full of students, you typically don't have the luxury of being able to explore tangents, because what interests one student won't interest everyone. However, mentoring someone gives you the space to explore tangents with your mentee. If she or he asks a question about something not directly related to the topic, you have the freedom to stop what you're doing and explore it. After all, you are the expert on your student.

Similarly, if a student's response to a question leads in an unexpected direction, you have the freedom to explore that as well. That said, just because you have the freedom to explore tangents doesn't necessarily mean that you should. To help you discern whether or not a tangent is worth exploring with your mentee, consider these questions:

1. Is the tangent still related to faith? If so, there's often value in exploring it.

2. If you avoid the tangent in order to reengage the topic at hand, will the student do so? Teens ask questions and talk about things that matter to them. As a result,

once something has been vocalized, teens may not be willing to resume your previous conversation until you've dealt with the matter at hand.

3. Will exploring the tangent together help you build trust with your mentee? If so, then it's likely worth exploring.

Remember, you have the content to create an hour-long discussion with your mentee that will help form her or his faith. However, the success of your mentoring meetings isn't measured by how much of the material you process. It's measured by the quality of your conversation. So, if talking about a tangent ends up in a quality discussion, do it, even if it means skipping some of the lesson material.

Lesson Summary

The final leg of this journey is understanding that it's not the end of the road and that more lies ahead in our walk with God. The final lesson of *Affirm* reminded students that hearing God often means listening to the words of others, sometimes even strangers.

The anchor point for this lesson was Genesis 24:57-58:

"They said, 'Summon the young woman, and let's ask her opinion.' They called Rebekah and said to her, 'Will you go with this man?'"

"She said, 'I will go.'"

Catch-up Questions

To catch up with your mentee this week, use this prompt:

Tell me about a friend with whom you were close but now you've lost touch. What made you grow apart? What would it take to renew a friendship with this person? Would you want to renew the friendship? Why or why not?

Once your mentee has answered this prompt, share your own response.

Discussion Questions

In their journals this week, students were asked to write an affirmation of faith. You might find it beneficial to use part of your mentoring meeting to ask your mentee to share his or her affirmation of faith with you. Then process the experience of writing it using questions like:

- Was it easy or hard to write your affirmation of faith? Why?

- Had you been asked to write your affirmation of faith two years ago, how do you think it would have differed from the one you wrote today?

- Two years from now, what do you hope will still be true of your affirmation of faith? Why?

- Why is the practice of writing an affirmation of faith important?

Other questions you can use this week during your mentoring meeting include:

1. What does it mean to you to hear God speak?

2. What are some of the common ways in which God speaks today?

3. How do you know whether or not what you hear is God?

4. Read 1 Samuel 3:1-5. Who does Samuel think is calling him? Why?

5. Why do you think Samuel is unable to recognize God's voice when he hears it?

6. Read 1 Samuel 3:6-7. According to verse 7, "Samuel didn't yet know the LORD." To you, what does it mean to know the Lord?

7. How well do you think you have to "know the Lord" before you can recognize the Lord's voice? What, if anything, can you do in order to better know the Lord?

8. When, if ever, has it been difficult for you to recognize God's voice? Why do you think you were unable to recognize God's voice in that moment?

9. Read 1 Samuel 3:8-9. Why do you think Eli, Samuel's older and wiser mentor and priest, was able to recognize the Lord's call before Samuel?

10. How might a mentor help you hear and recognize God's call on your life?

11. What does it mean to you to be called by God?

12. In his book *Wishful Thinking*, Frederick Buchner says, "The place God calls you to is the place where your deep gladness and the world's deep hunger meet."[1] What do you do that brings you joy?

    a. Look around you. What needs do you see in your family? school? community? church? world?

    b. How could you use the things that bring you joy to meet the needs you just identified in your daily life and world? Could it be that God is calling you to meet some of those needs right now? Why or why not?

13. How might God's call for you change in the days and years ahead?

14. Read 1 Samuel 3:9-10. In order to hear God, you must be ready to listen to God. What spiritual practices will prepare you to hear God's call on your life?

15. What have you learned about your faith in Christ through participating in *Affirm*?

Closing Prayer

This week, as you close in prayer:

- Thank God for your mentee.

- Thank God for the relationship you've begun to form with your mentee. Ask God to continue to grow this relationship deeper.

- Pray for your mentee's ability to listen to and hear God speak in his or her life.

- Pray that God would surround your mentee with mentors who will help him or her discern God's voice and God's call.

- Pray for your mentee to continue wrestling with God's call, right here and right now.

- Ask God to give your mentee the courage to do whatever God is calling him or her to do.

Once you've prayed for your mentee, give him or her the opportunity to pray for you also!

---

[1] See *https://www.goodreads.com/quotes/140448-the-place-God-calls-you-to-is-the-place-where*

Life After Affirm

You made it!

Thank you for investing in your teen's life throughout *Affirm*. Thank you for meeting weekly with your mentee, praying for him or her throughout the week, sharing vulnerably from your own life, and caring. As your formal time of mentoring comes to a close, it's only natural to wonder what's next for you and your mentee. At this point in time, you have two options. You can end your formal mentoring time together and continue investing in your mentee informally, or you can continue in a formal mentoring relationship.

Tips for Beginning an Informal Mentoring Relationship with Your Mentee

Now that you've completed this curriculum, it's OK to end your formal mentoring relationship with your teen for a variety of reasons. You fulfilled your commitment so it might be a natural time to move on. You may have faithfully invested in your mentee but lacked any real chemistry between the two of you. Or, you may have hit it off with your mentee but feel that time wise, you cannot continue in a formal mentoring relationship.

Whatever the reason for ending your formal mentoring relationship, know that it's OK. However, even though you're ending your formal mentoring relationship, we hope you'll continue investing in your teen informally. After all, over the last several weeks, you've become part of this teen's circle of champions. So, please continue. Here are five practical ideas for investing in your mentee informally.

1. Continue to pray for your mentee regularly. Occasionally send a note of encouragement in the mail to remind the student you're praying for him or her.

2. Seek out your mentee in church on a regular basis. Do more than say, "hi." Stop and talk about what's going on in his or her life. Then follow up the next week.

3. During the course of your formal mentoring relationship, you got to know your mentee. You know what he or she cares about as well as his or her interests. So, show up for those things. Attend a game, a concert, or an extracurricular event. Be his or her champion!

4. Continue to hold your mentee accountable for the practices he or she was interested in starting in the faith journey. Give grace when needed and be a cheerleader for making strides in the faith.

5. Schedule an impromptu check-in meeting, even if you can't commit to mentoring your teen regularly. Meet for coffee and catch up on progress in life and faith. Spend time in prayer together. Ideal times for this checkup might be at one month and six months after your formal mentoring relationship ends.

Practical Ideas for How to Continue Formally Mentoring Your Mentee

For a variety of reasons, you might find that it makes sense to continue your formal mentoring relationship with your mentee even after *Affirm* ends. If both you and your mentee are interested in continuing to meet formally, simply model your meeting times after what you've been doing. In place of discussion questions, here are three options for what you can continue exploring.

1. Read and discuss a book of the Bible together. If you don't know where to start, consider the Gospel of Mark, which is short and action-packed. Read a chapter (or a section) a week. Spend your time together answering your mentee's questions, wrestling with how you see yourself in the story, and finding ways to apply the story to your life.

2. Read and discuss a Christian book together a chapter at a time. A few great books to read with teens include *Love Does* by Bob Goff, *Messy Spirituality* by Mike Yaconelli, and *The Irresistible Revolution* by Shane Claiborne.

3. Discuss the previous week's sermon and the corresponding Bible passage. During the sermon, make note of a few things you found interesting, questions that arise, and ideas about which you disagree. Discuss these with your mentee.

Ending Well

Regardless of whether you decide to continue investing in your mentee formally or informally, make sure you end your time together in a positive way. Thank your mentee for trusting you with her or his story. Tell your mentee what you learned from her or him.

If you plan on continuing a formal mentoring relationship, decide what you'll do next and how often you'll meet. If you opt to continue a more informal mentoring relationship, let your mentee know when and how to connect with you.

Know that your time as a mentor mattered. You shared God's good news as well as your life with a student. You cared for a student in a very real and tangible way.

For that, we thank you.

CPSIA information can be obtained
at www.ICGtesting.com
Printed in the USA
LVHW03s2312060718
582846LV00002B/2/P